Alexandr Vasilievich Tolmachev

Digger philosophy and the hollow earth theory

Alexandr Vasilievich Tolmachev

Digger philosophy and the hollow earth theory

collection of scientific articles

ScienciaScripts

Imprint

Any brand names and product names mentioned in this book are subject to trademark, brand or patent protection and are trademarks or registered trademarks of their respective holders. The use of brand names, product names, common names, trade names, product descriptions etc. even without a particular marking in this work is in no way to be construed to mean that such names may be regarded as unrestricted in respect of trademark and brand protection legislation and could thus be used by anyone.

Cover image: www.ingimage.com

This book is a translation from the original published under ISBN 978-620-4-75225-9.

Publisher:
Sciencia Scripts
is a trademark of
Dodo Books Indian Ocean Ltd. and OmniScriptum S.R.L publishing group

120 High Road, East Finchley, London, N2 9ED, United Kingdom
Str. Armeneasca 28/1, office 1, Chisinau MD-2012, Republic of Moldova, Europe
Printed at: see last page
ISBN: 978-620-5-91001-6

A. V. Tolmachev

"DIGGER PHILOSOPHY AND THE HOLLOW EARTH THEORY"

(COLLECTION OF SCIENTIFIC ARTICLES)

Table of Contents

Introduction

The Digger Movement, which emerged in Russia in the 1980s and 1990s, aims to explore the underground spaces of cities. The Russian Digger Movement consists of various branches: research, rescue, treasure-hunting, neo-pagan, esoteric, excursion and tourism, etc. I offer a religious studies perspective on the religious and esoteric side of the Diggers movement.

Deep dungeons draw Diggers to test their mettle, to make new discoveries and even to meet unknown civilisations.

Contemporary diggerism is a youth subculture. In Moscow, diggers offer journeys and excursions through quarries and caves, along underground rivers, and the dungeons of old monasteries and fortresses. However, Diggers need their own mythology, legends and even a kind of quasi-religion. Therefore ideas arise about the emergence of digger heroes capable of unlocking the ancient secrets of the underworld.

The leader of the Russian Diggers, Vadim Vyacheslavovich Mikhailov, founder and leader of the international and Russian Diggers movement, founder and president of the Diggers Planet Underground Research Centre, is considered to be the founder of the Digger philosophy of the "Inner World".

The philosophy of the 'Inner World', according to Vadim Mikhailov, is 'the foundation and concentrator of modern human life' in the context of underground space and underground time. The foundation for this philosophy is the idea of our planet as the Hollow Earth.

Among the most significant works on the Hollow Earth theory, in my opinion, are: W. J. Emerson's "The Smoked God or

Journey to the Inner World". J. J. Emerson's "The Soiled God, or Journey into the Inner World", J. W. Lloyd's "Etidorpa or the Edge of the Earth. A Strange Story of a Mysterious Being', and the Russian military researcher Leonid Ivashov's 'The Tilted World'.

The physical and mathematical basis of the Hollow Earth theory is based on the fundamental statements of mathematics, non-classical physics, I. Prigozhin's theory of self-organisation, internal time hierarchy, the generalised theory of order and chaos.

The religious, or rather quasi-religious side of the Hollow Earth theory manifests itself in connection with information coming from contact persons who have voluntarily or involuntarily come into contact with "aliens" from other inner earth worlds, and which contain certain instructions, predictions, foresight or prophecies.

Among Moscow's Diggers, according to their leader, almost all are Orthodox Christians. There is no place for non-believing atheists underground, says Mikhailov. They never go underground without collective and individual prayers to their patrons and protectors - Archangel Michael and St. Nicholas the Wonderworker. Vadim Mikhailov told me that in critical moments underground, when a digger's life hangs in the balance, only a loud prayer appeal to Archangel Michael has saved them more than once.

The Diggers are convinced that the Hollow Earth Theory, together with the philosophy of the "Inner World", is a science, a myth, an emerging religious cult, esoteric knowledge, as well as a break through the veils of any religious cult to the Creator, to the Cosmos, to the living planet Earth, to the human spirit and souls of all living beings, and most importantly - one of the ways to human self-organisation in the living world.

1. *A. V. Tolmachev* **Religious studies of Tolkien occult mythology in the subculture of Russian Diggers.**

(article for the Round Table "The Theory of Occultation: Meaning, Applications, Perspectives", Moscow, AIEM, 2022, 24 May)

Annotation:

The movement of Russian diggers consists of different directions: research; rescue; treasure hunting; neo-pagan; religious and esoteric; excursion and tourism, etc. I offer a religious studies perspective on the religious-esoteric side of the Diggers movement and especially on the esoteric and occult side of Diggerism. Religious studies help us better discern Diggerism from a synthesis of mythological cognition with scientific, religious, and intuitive approaches to the study of the peculiarities of the Russian Diggers movement.

Contemporary diggerism is a youth subculture. In Moscow, diggers offer journeys and excursions through quarries and caves, along underground rivers, and the dungeons of old monasteries and fortresses. However, Diggers need their own mythology, legends and even a kind of quasi-religion. Therefore ideas arise about the emergence of digger heroes capable of unlocking the ancient secrets of the underworld.

Russian digger leader Vadim Mikhailov, founder and president of the Diggers of Planet Underground Research Centre, is considered to be the founder of the "Inner World" digger philosophy.

The philosophy of the 'Inner World', according to Vadim Mikhailov, is 'the foundation and concentrator of modern human life' in the context of underground space and underground time. The foundation for this philosophy was the idea of our planet as the Hollow Earth.

Among the most significant works on the Hollow Earth theory are, in my opinion. J. J. Emerson's "The Soiled God, or Journey into the Inner World", J. W. Lloyd's "Etidorpa or the Edge of the Earth. A Strange Story of a Mysterious Being', and the Russian military researcher Leonid Ivashov's 'The Tumbledown World'.

Esoterism in the modern digger movement is becoming one of the methodological principles for rethinking earlier scientific knowledge, as well as a useful source of new knowledge about the unity of materialistic and spiritual knowledge of nature and man, especially in the complex conditions of the underworld.

The philosophy of the Diggers' Inner World is closely connected with the new emerging mythology, modern mythological works in verse and prose, especially works in the fantasy genre. Fantasy in the study of religion is seen, on the one hand, as a kind of experimental myth-constructing science and, on the other hand, as a quasi-religious mystery belief in the cosmic predestination of human life. The fantasy genre is impossible without religious, mythological, scientific and intuitive knowledge; it was born out of people's mythological and religious worldview.

The fantasy of J.R.R. Tolkien, deeply revered among Diggers, is akin not only to Celtic and Scandinavian mythologies, but also to the Slavic religious and mythological system. Take for example the way of the Hobbit, but not the way drawn on a map of Middle-earth in geographical space. The way of the Hobbit is an ancient Slavic mystical "Way of the Fool", i.e. the way of revealing wisdom that transcends the ordinary and profane, but leads to the sacred. This path was followed by Ivanushka the Fool from Russian folk tales, as well as by the "mad sage" Khoja Nasreddin from Sufi proverbs.

J.R.R. Tolkien's myth-making with The Lord of the Rings and The Hobbit was the best example of Christian and pseudo-Christian myth-making. They are not science fiction and not just fantasies about the created world of Arda with Middle-earth and the Immortal Lands, with its development, life and overcoming colossal difficulties. They are myths about the free choice of peoples and individuals to follow the path of Love and with the energy of Love not for personal gain or consumer saturation, and not with the help of some super-divine stills, but for the benefit of all peoples and with their own courage.

Why have the works of J.R.R. Tolkien become incredibly popular in Russia among ordinary people, as well as among diggers? Perhaps because they are not just works of fiction, but a whole sacred mythology which people feel like the living world of Arda and Middle-earth. Many people on the planet and in Russia itself have intuitively felt this living world. Tolkien's mythology has been felt by many people as real, living and sacred, something like some kind of divine revelation. And something similar could be found in medieval Christian mystics, who through divine revelations showed medieval man the worldview of true Christians. These included the Orthodox Hesychists, the great Dante and his Divine Comedy, and the "Teutonic philosopher" Jakob Böhme.

Mythology, unlike religious doctrines, does not teach man to build a relationship with deity and death. The mythological consciousness of man already contains knowledge about deity and death. Mythology helps man to structure his social life. Myth is a kind of icon in Christianity - a symbolic concentration of faith in folk religion and mythology.

J.R.R. Tolkien once expressed the crucial idea that man has the right to create, to create "Secondary worlds", because he himself was created in the image and likeness of the Creator of Heaven and Earth. "My world came into being with me - although this is of no interest to anyone except myself. I mean, not a day goes by that I don't keep making it up." "But Man is the Creator. The Way of Creation is open to Him. And Man speaks according to ancient and divine laws - Thus has the Creator the Original created him."

The virtual space of Tolkien's mythical worlds is structured on the basis of the attributes that allow to consider the Secondary World as a certain system of reference points: the system of "centre" - "periphery" relations; perceptions of physical properties of space (further - closer, higher - lower, etc.).The following are the parameters of object localisation in virtual space - types of spatial visions (map-view and map-way); projection of toponyms through the concept of "friend-or-foe"; comprehension of "friend" against "foe"; "detachment" of "friend" and making "personal" of "foe".

Diggers, admirers of J. R. R. Tolkien's myth-making, believe that it is sacred because any mythologically minded person has a special religious-mythological sense, a certain inner "tuning fork" for tuning into sacred myths rather than into simulacra. J.R.R. Tolkien's virtual space, from the Diggers' point of view, is a mythological space where heroes constantly make a free choice to follow the path of Love and with the energy of Love not for personal gain, but for the benefit of all peoples of Middle-earth, relying upon their own courage and upon the help of divine powers. It is this mythology with its belief in magical practices of elemental control and reliance on the philosophy of the "Inner World" that helps Diggers not only to survive in the dungeons, but also to make new discoveries and transform their own spirits there.

Keywords: Diggers, Tolkien, myth, religion, esoterism, occultism, subculture.

Introduction.

Young people want to make discoveries. And while practically the entire surface of the planet has been explored and mapped, underground spaces still harbour unknowns. The Movement of Diggers, which emerged in Russia in the 1980s and 1990s, set out to explore the underground spaces of cities. The movement of Russian diggers consists of various directions: research, rescue, treasure-hunting, neo-pagan, esoteric, excursion and tourist and others. I offer a religious studies perspective on the religious and esoteric side of the Diggers movement.

Diggers, meaning 'diggers', are people fond of exploring man-made underground structures, although this was also the name given to members of the poor peasantry during the English Revolution, who fought against private land ownership in the mid-17th century.

Digging, i.e. the activity of exploring the underground structures of cities, emerged in the late 19th and early 20th centuries as a branch of speleology. The first diggers were archaeologists, excavating forgotten dungeons for the purpose of their historical investigation. Modern diggers are, of course, nothing to do with archaeology. They are drawn to dungeons by a different kind of passion, which can be explained in terms of their acquisition of esoteric knowledge and the application of occult techniques.

Religious studies help us better discern Diggerism from a synthesis of mythological cognition with scientific, religious, and intuitive approaches to the study of the peculiarities of the Russian Diggers movement. In this paper I will be interested in the esoteric and occult sides of diggerism. For a long time the terms 'esotericism' and 'occultism' were used interchangeably, but today they have been separated by understanding esotericism as theoretical constructions and occultism as astrological, magical, alchemical and other practices involving secret or hidden forces of nature or the cosmos, which cannot be measured and understood by modern science.

1.Esoterism and occult practices - Diggers' ways of knowing the underground worlds.

For a long time the terms "esotericism" and "occultism" were used interchangeably, but today some researchers have begun to separate them, understanding by esotericism theoretical constructions and by occultism astrological, magical, alchemical and other practices involving secret or hidden forces of nature or the cosmos, and which cannot be measured and understood by means of modern science.

In the system of esoteric knowledge there is a particular classification. For example, alchemy dealing with obtaining gold, composing preparations and potions, pills of immortality - is called external alchemy; and transmutation of the spirit, achievement of absolute health or even immortality - is called internal alchemy. Perhaps the transmutation of one's own spirit is the most attractive aspect of digging.

In J.W. Lloyd's diggers' board book, Etidorpa or the End of the Earth. The Strange Story of a Mysterious Being', in his description of his descent into the deep underground, as far back as the nineteenth century, states the following: 'It seemed to me that my stamina to bear fatigue increased to an astonishing degree... My companion replied that the atmosphere of the cave had an inherent animating power, neutralising fatigue, or - as he put it - 'there is an innate organic energy, coming from an active gaseous substance belonging to the air of the cave at this depth. It sustains vitality through distribution directly to its preservation, taking the place of food and drink" ... "You do not understand how ordinary air sustains the mind and animates the muscles, and at the same time is carried away from the muscles and all other tissues. There are facts that are not satisfactorily explained by scientific statements, this includes oxygen enrichment of the blood. As we descend underground, we will find an increase in the vitality of the cave atmosphere"..." [*Lloyd, 2009, pp. 74-75*].

Deep dungeons draw Diggers to test their mettle, to make new discoveries and even to meet unknown civilisations.

Contemporary diggerism is a youth subculture. In Moscow, diggers offer journeys and excursions through quarries and caves, along underground rivers, and the dungeons of old monasteries and fortresses. However, Diggers need their own mythology, legends and even a kind of quasi-religion. Therefore ideas arise about the emergence of digger heroes capable of unlocking the ancient secrets of the underworld.

Vadim Vyacheslavovich Mikhailov, the leader of the Russian and international "Diggers" movement, is the founder and president of the Diggers Planet Underground Research Centre, and is considered to be the founder of the "Inner World" Digger Philosophy.

The philosophy of the 'Inner World', according to Vadim Mikhailov, is 'the foundation and concentrator of modern human life' in the conditions of underground space and underground time. The foundation for this philosophy is the idea of our planet as the Hollow Earth.

Among the most significant works on the Hollow Earth theory are, in my opinion. J. J. Emerson's "The Soiled God, or Journey into the Inner World", J. W. Lloyd's "Etidorpa or the Edge of the Earth. A Strange Story of a Mysterious Being', and the Russian military researcher Leonid Ivashov's 'The Overturned World'.

Esoterism in the modern digger movement is becoming one of the methodological principles for rethinking earlier scientific knowledge, as well as a useful source of new knowledge about the unity of materialistic and spiritual knowledge of nature and man, especially in the complex conditions of the underworld.

2.Digger mythology and the myth-making of J.R.R. Tolkien.

The philosophy of the Diggers' Inner World is closely connected with the new emerging mythology, modern mythological works in verse and prose, especially works in the fantasy genre. Fantasy in the study of religion is considered, on the one hand, as a kind of experimental myth-constructing science and, on the other hand, as a quasi-religious mystery belief in the cosmic predestination of human life. The fantasy genre is impossible without religious, mythological, scientific and intuitive knowledge; it was born out of the mythological and religious worldview of people.

The fantasy of J.R.R. Tolkien, deeply revered among Diggers, is akin not only to Celtic and Scandinavian mythologies, but also to Slavic religious and mythological systems. Take for example the way of the Hobbit, but not the way drawn on a map of Middle-earth in geographical space. The way of the Hobbit is an ancient Slavic mystical "Way of the Fool", i.e. the way of revealing wisdom that exceeds the ordinary and profane, but leads to the sacred. This path was followed by Ivanushka the Fool from Russian folk tales, as well as by the "mad sage" Khoja Nasreddin from Sufi proverbs.

J.R.R. Tolkien's myth-making with The Lord of the Rings and The Hobbit was the best example of Christian and pseudo-Christian myth-making. They are not science fiction and not just fantasies about the created world of Arda with Middle-earth and the Immortal Lands, with its development, life and overcoming colossal difficulties. They are myths about the free choice of peoples and individuals to follow the path of Love and with the energy of Love not for personal gain or consumer saturation, and not with the help of some super-divine stills, but for the benefit of all peoples and with their own courage.

Why have the works of J.R.R. Tolkien become incredibly popular in Russia among ordinary people, as well as among diggers? Perhaps because they are not just works of fiction, but a whole sacred mythology which people feel like the living world of Arda and Middle-earth. Many people on the planet and in Russia itself have intuitively felt this living world. Tolkien's mythology has been felt by many people as real, living and sacred, something like some kind of divine revelation. And something similar could be found in medieval Christian mystics, who through divine revelations showed medieval man the worldview of true Christians. The orthodox Hesychists and the great Dante with his Divine Comedy [2001] should also be referred to as such. [*Dante, 2001*], and the "Teutonic philosopher" Jakob Böhme [*Böhme, 2010*].

Diggers, admirers of J.R.R. Tolkien's myth-making, believe that it is sacred because any mythologically minded person has a special religious-mythological sense, a certain inner "tuning fork" for tuning into sacred myths rather than into simulacra. J.R.R. Tolkien's virtual space, from the Diggers' point of view, is a mythological space where heroes constantly make a free choice to follow the path of Love and with the energy of Love not for personal gain, but for the benefit of all peoples of Middle-earth, relying upon their own courage and upon the help of divine powers. It is this mythology with its belief in magical practices of elemental control and reliance on the Inner World philosophy that helps Diggers not only to survive in the dungeons, but also to make new discoveries and transform their own spirits there.

3.Digger Occultism and Esoterism in the Modern Age.

The religious, or rather quasi-religious side of the Hollow Earth theory manifests itself in connection with information coming from contact persons who have voluntarily or involuntarily come into contact with "aliens" from other inner earth worlds, and which contain certain instructions, predictions, foresight or prophecies.

The Italian philosopher Giovanni Pico della Mirandola (1463-1494) considered occult and natural magic practices that attracted the hidden forces of the cosmos. His first thesis from a corpus of "900 theses on dialectics, morals, physics, mathematics for public discussion" (1496) was as follows: "All that magic which is now employed, and which the Church quite deservedly eradicates, has no solidity, no foundation, no truth, since it comes from the enemies of the first truth, from the powers of darkness, who darken the disturbed mind with the darkness of falsehood."... 'Natural magic is permitted and not forbidden...'... 'Magic is a practical part of the natural sciences...'... 'Neither in heaven nor on earth are there such scattered and disparate beginnings that the magician cannot bring them into being and bring them together'... "To engage in magic is nothing less than to marry the world"... "Proceeding from the beginnings of an intimate philosophy, it must be admitted that in magical operations inscriptions and figures are far more powerful than material properties"." [*The Book of Magicians, 2009, pp. 71-73*].

The German philosopher, theologian, alchemist, physician, occultist and lawyer in one person - Agrippa of Nettesheim (1486 - 1535) formulated the very concept of occultism. He included astrology in a unified system of occult sciences. "In his three-volume work, On the Secret Philosophy, Agrippa of Nettesheims united all the occult sciences into a single system for the first time. In this work he set forth a doctrine of magic based on a view in the interconnectedness of all things, combining into a coherent system the secret knowledge - hermetics, magic and astrology - and linking the Neoplatonic and Kabbalistic teachings with them.... Agrippa's goal was to transform magic from a supernatural science to a natural one. Magical operations, he believed, should be incorporated into physics, mathematics and theology. Agrippa elevated the doctrine of mutual sympathy and antipathy to a universal law of nature." [*The Book of Magicians, 2009, p. 94*].

Esoterism in modern times becomes one of the methodological principles of rethinking previously obtained scientific knowledge, as well as a useful source of new knowledge about the unity of materialistic and spiritual cognition of nature and man. F.R. Hantseverov reflects on scientific cognition of natural phenomena: "It is known, that the classical natural-scientific knowledge developed, though quite powerful toolkit, but suitable for scientific study and interpretation only of 'classical phenomena' of physical world. Outside it was the entire field of unrecognised, so-called paranormal phenomena.

Therefore world parapsychology as a whole, including astrology, ufology, biolocation, and other directions, is now busy creating a conceptual framework for their research. And this activity of searching for a methodological and theoretical platform and its introduction into practice has, unlike in the past, a significant impact on the effectiveness of ongoing research in these non-traditional fields". [*Hantseverov, 1999, p. 23]*

Hall Manley P. reports that "back in the days when Hermes walked the earth with men, he entrusted his followers with the sacred 'Book of Thoth'. This book contains the secrets of the process by which the rebirth of mankind can be realised... When certain parts of the brain are stimulated by secret processes in the mysteries, man's consciousness expands and he is allowed to see the Immortals and be close to the higher deities. "The Book of Thoth describes the method by which such stimulation can be achieved." [*Hall, 2019, p. 125*].

All esoteric knowledge is built on the postulate of the likeness of microcosm and macrocosm, and therefore it is possible for man to influence nature and nature to influence man. For example, alchemy forms notions that as a result of the interaction of qualitative principles (initials) and states of the primordial elements any transmutation of material substances and transmutation of the human spirit can be performed.

In religious studies of Digger philosophy, magical rituals, ritual actions, and incantations are seen as a way of influencing the natural and divine forces of the underworld, which can help bring about mystical creation, i.e. the transmutation of the Digger spirit.

The task of various esoteric concepts is similar to the tasks of religious and mythological concepts - to bring order to society, to an order of a higher level than that experienced by man at the moment. In the language of modern physics, in all known periods of life of human society there is a growth of entropy of human society, i.e. fall of vital order and increase of chaos. Science, religion, mythology, esoterics - all of them give man tools to order his life, reduce entropy and increase structural order of human society.

The brilliant work of the great Russian mystic of the 20th century Daniel Andreev "The Rose of the World". [*Andreev, 2006*] forms one's idea of an infinite number of intelligent worlds in the multidimensional (space-time) life of the living universe and the living planet. The Rose of the World structures the worlds of angels and the worlds of demons; points to the role of Christ, Holy Sophia and the choice of free man in creating new worlds and preserving life in all worlds; explains the cruel laws of death and "natural" selection as compromise laws between the forces of Light and the forces of Darkness Noting the outstanding role of Sophia the Wisdom of God in collaboration and cooperation with believers of different religious faiths in the creation of a new all-planetary all-Christian religion for the last struggle of mankind against the Antichrist. Such a struggle in the philosophy of the Diggers is accepted as proper and takes place during every dive into the underworlds. Prayers and magical rites are a must for the Diggers. They believe it is the only way to be prepared for encounters with unfriendly underground forces and demonic energies.

4. Diggers' reinterpretation of mythology and the emerging religious cult in J.R.R. Tolkien's worlds.

A certain connection of J.R.R. Tolkien's mythology with the astral religion of the ancients should be noted. In the astral religion of the ancients the world of deities is the world of stars and planets. Man, gazing into the sky, recognises his planetary deity, a star deity - a star protector, a protector spirit who helps him all his life (like knowing the name of his guardian angel in Christianity). The connection of the Tolkien mythological epochs can be divided into three phases similar to the three phases of ancient astral religion: a) The eras of the Creation of Arda and the Settlement of Arda are comparable to the stage of Old Babylonian Sumerian star religion about the creation of the solar system and the Earth, and are connected with the mythology of omens; b) The eras of Luminaries, the Trees of Darkness, the Stars are comparable to the stage of Zoroastrianism and Orphism in star religion, and connected with the opposition between the creating and destructive beginnings; c) The ages of the Sun are comparable to the stage originating from late Zoroastrianism in star religion, namely the worship of Heaven and the belief in the transmigration of souls of dead people passing through three worlds (world of good thought, world of good words, world of good deeds) to the bright world of Ahura-Mazda. In later versions of Zoroastrian star religion the three worlds (regions) are replaced by the seven heavens or planetary spheres and the belief that a person's destiny is determined by the location of the stars at birth.

This exactly repeats the Zoroastrian and Zurvanite notions of the distortion of the created world.   P.P. Globa reports that "according to the "Bundahishnu" during the invasion of the Evil Spirit into the Universe "planets with many demons broke through the heavenly sphere, and they mixed the constellations; and the entire Universe was disfigured as if fire disfigured every place, and smoke rose over it". [*Globa, 2007, pp. 369-370*]

Publicity and aesthetic pluralism contributed to the diversity of approaches in the assimilation of J.R.R. Tolkien's legacy within the framework of the Russian literary system. Reception of J.R.R. Tolkien's texts includes the emergence of many mythological and simply artistic variations on the themes of J.R.R. Tolkien's works.

The texts of the works themselves became the source of the Tolkien subculture. The multifaceted nature of the influence of J.R.R. Tolkien's legacy on Russian literature and culture necessitates a comprehensive approach to its study, taking into account both the literary and socio-cultural situation.

The life of J.R.R. Tolkien's works themselves in the Russian language space is determined by the literary experience, aesthetic perceptions and intuitive expectations of Russian recipients.

Such famous recipients in Russia have been, for example, Nick Perumov (The Elven Blade, Black Arrow, Hannah's Adamant), and less well-known are dozens of writers and poets. The Diggers are not far behind. For example, their leader Vadim Mikhailov is the author and performer of around two thousand of his own poems and songs.

J.R.R. Tolkien's Legendarium, which reflects his artistic conception, demonstrates a certain representation of incompleteness, but not so much formal as substantive. Such a legendarium appears as a time-varying phenomenon, and therefore potentially allowing for further refinement as well.

Mircea Eliade said that "Myth recounts a sacral story, a narrative of an event that took place at the memorable time of the 'beginning of all beginnings'. Myth tells how reality, thanks to the exploits of supernatural beings, reached its incarnation and realisation...". [*Eliade, 2010, p. 29*] Roland Barthes said about myth that it aims at changing reality and creates an image of reality that would coincide with value expectations, that myth conceals its ideological character, and that myth is not a relic of archaic consciousness, but part of modern culture.

And if "Tolkien's greatest passion and main goal in life was to create a coherent mythological system for the English." [*Dey, 2003, p. 8*], then for the new Russian writers who have taken up the baton in creating further lives of Tolkien's mythological worlds, the reception of J.R.R. Tolkien's work also allows the creation of a new Russian mythology, including the mythology of Diggers.

Mythology, unlike religious doctrines, does not teach man to build a relationship with deity and death. The mythological consciousness of man already contains knowledge about deity and death. Mythology helps man to structure his social life. Myth is a kind of icon in Christianity - a symbolic concentration of faith in folk religion and mythology.

J.R.R. Tolkien once expressed the crucial idea that man has the right to create, to create "Secondary worlds", because he himself was created in the image and likeness of the Creator of Heaven and Earth. "My world came into being with me - although this is of no interest to anyone except myself. I mean, not a day goes by that I don't keep making it up." "But Man is the Creator. The Way of Creation is open to Him. And Man speaks according to ancient and divine laws - Thus has the Creator the Original created him."

The virtual space of J.R.R. Tolkien's mythical worlds is structured by Diggers on the basis of the attributes that allow to consider the Secondary World as a certain system of reference points: the system of "centre" - "periphery" relations; perceptions of physical properties of space (further - closer, higher - lower, etc.); parameters of the object's localization in virtual space - types of spatial visions (map-viewing - map-way; projection of toponyms through the concept of "our own" - "alien"; and the concept of the object's location in virtual space.The system of relations of the type "centre - periphery"; perceptions of the physical properties of space (further - closer - higher - lower, etc.); parameters for localising an object in virtual space - types of spatial visions (map-view and map-way); projection of toponyms through the concept "friend-or-foe"; comprehension of "friend" against "stranger"; "detachment" of "friend" and making "personal" of "stranger".

Diggers' study of J.R.R. Tolkien's virtual space allows not only to consider his Secondary world as a whole, but also to see the projection of world history and culture within the virtual space of "The Hobbit" and "The Lord of the Rings". For example, the study of the Theponymicope of "The Lord of the Rings", taking into account the meanings of its units, allows to understand the geographical proper name as a coiled cultural and historical text.

By creating a fictional reality, Tolkien programs axiological orientation in it as one of the most important components of his characters' world model. J.R.R. Tolkien conceives the space of his myth as a kind of extension, an orientation field; the mythical surface surrounding his characters, interacting with the characters, participates in the development of the action, is filled with supernatural phenomena, on it and in it unfolds events understood in retrospect as the history of Eurasia.

Great thinkers and writers like J.R.R. Tolkien, who are illuminated by a divine spark, are capable of creating living mythical worlds. Such living worlds always require self-development and continuation of their subsequent eternal creation by other thinkers with divine love and help from the Creator in new virtual spaces.

The Diggers are convinced that the Hollow Earth Theory, together with the philosophy of the "Inner World" and Tolkien's reinterpreted Legendarium, is a science, a myth, an emerging religious cult, esoteric knowledge, as well as a break through the veils of any religious cult to the Creator, to the Cosmos, to the living planet Earth, to the human spirit and souls of all living beings, and most importantly - one of the ways to human self-organisation in the living world.

Self-organisation of man, the Diggers themselves and the entire living world destroys the artificial world, because it is only possible in the living world when living creative energy is received from ."nowhere" (as atheist philosophers explain), from resonance (as physicists explain), from the divine grace of the Holy Spirit (as theologians explain).

List of references:

1. Andreev, D.L. Selected Works in 2 vols. vols. 1: The Rose of the World. Metaphysical treatise. / D.L. Andreev - M.: Arda. 2006. - 592 с.

2. Böhme, J. Aurora, or the morning star in ascension. / J. Böhme - M.: Amphora. 2018. - 512 с.

3. Globa P. P. The teachings of the ancient Aryans. / P.P. Globa - M.: Eksmo, Yauza, 2007. - 752 с. - ISBN 978-5-699-22713-6.

4. Dante, Alighieri The Divine Comedy. / A. Dante - M.: Amphora. 2018. - 512 с.

5. Day, D. Tolkien's Worlds: The Big Illustrated Encyclopedia / D. Day / translated from English by M. Vinogradova, S. Likhacheva, S. Taskaeva - M.: Egmont Russia Ltd. 2003.

6. Ivashov L. Overturned world / Leonid Ivashov - M.: Publishing house Argumenty Nedeli, 2020. - 384 с. ISBN 978-5-6043544-1-4.

7. The Book of Magicians / co-creator. V. Rokhmistrova - SPb.: Amfora, TID Amfora. 2009. - 314 c. ISBN 978-5-367-01024-4.

8. Lloyd J.W. Etidorhpa or the End of the Earth. The strange story of a mysterious creature (Etidorhpa The End of Earth. The man who did it, 1895) / J. W. Lloyd / translated from English by N. Bugaenko - Toronto, 2009. - 244 c. - ill. - (http://www.myshambhala.com).

9. Tolkien J.R.R. The Hobbit, or There and Back Again. The Lord of the Rings / J.R.R. Tolkien / translated from English by N.Rahmanova, N.Grigorieva, V.Grushetsky. - SPb: The ABC-Classic, 2004. - 1136 c. ISBN 5-352-00184-9.

10. Tolmachev A. V. Philosophy of Space and Time: Human Evolution in a Changing System of Space-time Coordinates. Part 1. / A. V. Tolmachev - Chisinau, Moldova - EU: LAP Lambert Academic Publishing, 2021, - 150 p. ISBN 978-620-4-18152-3.

11. Hantseverov F. R. Eniology: miracles without mysticism. Book of Scientific Versions / F.R. Hantseverov - M.: International Academy of Energy and Information Sciences. ASM, 1999. - 445 c. ISBN 5-900576-08-6.

12. Hall Manley P. The Secret Teachings: An Encyclopaedic Statement of Hermetic, Kabbalistic and Rosencreutzian Symbolic Philosophy / Manley P. Hall / translated from English by V.V. Tselischeva. - M.: KoLibri, Azbuka-Attikus, 2019. - 960 p.: ill. ISBN 978-5-389-13333-4.

13. Eliade, M. Aspects of myth / M. Eliade // translated from French by V. P. Bolshakov. P. Bolshakov. - M.: Academic Prekt. 2010. - 251 c. - ISBN 978-5-8291-1125-0.

14. Emerson W. J. J. The Smoky God or a Voyage to the Inner World, 1908 / W. J. Emerson / translated by E. Lavretskaya,

2013. J. Emerson / translated from English by E. Lavretskaya, 2013. - www.tempelvril.org.

2. *A. V. Tolmachev* **A Religious Studies perspective on the religious and esoteric philosophy of the "Inner World" of Russian Diggers.**

(article for the V Congress of the "Russian Society for Religious Studies" "Religion A Priori and A Posteriori", Kaliningrad, Immanuel Kant Federal University, 2022, 14-15 October).

Annotation.

The Digger Movement, which emerged in Russia in the 1980s and 1990s, aims to explore the underground spaces of cities. The Russian Digger Movement consists of various branches: research, rescue, treasure-hunting, neopaganism, esotericism, excursion and tourism, and others. I offer a religious studies perspective on the religious and esoteric side of the Diggers movement.

Deep dungeons draw Diggers to test their strength of character, as well as to make new discoveries and even to meet unknown civilisations.

Contemporary diggerism is a youth subculture. In Moscow, diggers offer journeys and excursions through quarries and caves, along underground rivers, and the dungeons of old monasteries and fortresses. However, Diggers need their own mythology, legends and even a kind of quasi-religion. Therefore ideas arise about the emergence of digger heroes capable of unlocking the ancient secrets of the underworld.

The leader of the Russian Diggers, Vadim Vyacheslavovich Mikhailov, founder and leader of the international and Russian Diggers movement, founder and president of the Diggers of the Planet Underground Research Centre, is considered to be the founder of the Digger philosophy of the "Inner World".

The Inner World philosophy, according to Vadim Mikhailov, is "the foundation and concentrator of modern human life" in the context of underground space and underground time.

The basis for this philosophy is the idea of our planet as the Hollow Earth.

Among the most significant works on the Hollow Earth theory, in my opinion, are: W. J. Emerson's "The Smoked God or Journey to the Inner World". J. J. Emerson's "The Soiled God, or Journey into the Inner World", J. W. Lloyd's "Etidorpa or the Edge of the Earth. A Strange Story of a Mysterious Being', and the Russian military researcher Leonid Ivashov's 'The Tilted World'.

The physical and mathematical basis of the Hollow Earth theory is based on the fundamental statements of mathematics, non-classical physics, I. Prigozhin's theory of self-organisation, internal time hierarchy, the generalised theory of order and chaos.

The religious, or rather quasi-religious side of the Hollow Earth theory manifests itself in connection with information coming from contact persons who have voluntarily or involuntarily come into contact with "aliens" from other inner earth worlds, and which contain certain instructions, predictions, foresight or prophecies.

Among Moscow's Diggers, according to their leader, almost all are Orthodox Christians. There is no place for non-believing atheists underground, says Mikhailov. They never go underground without collective and individual prayers to their patrons and protectors - Archangel Michael and St. Nicholas the Wonderworker. Vadim Mikhailov told me that in critical moments underground, when a digger's life hangs in the balance, only a loud prayer appeal to Archangel Michael has saved them more than once.

The Diggers are convinced that the Hollow Earth Theory, together with the philosophy of the "Inner World", is a science, a myth, an emerging religious cult, esoteric knowledge, as well as a break through the veils of any religious cult to the Creator, to the Cosmos, to the living planet Earth, to the human spirit and souls of all living beings, and most importantly - one of the ways to human self-organisation in the living world.

Keywords: digger, Christianity, esoterism, Hollow Earth.

Introduction.

Young people want to make discoveries. And while practically the entire surface of the planet has been explored and mapped, underground spaces still harbour unknowns. The Movement of Diggers, which emerged in Russia in the 1980s and 1990s, set out to explore the underground spaces of cities. The movement of Russian diggers consists of various directions: research, rescue, treasure-hunting, neo-pagan, esoteric, excursion and tourist and others. I offer a religious studies perspective on the religious and esoteric side of the Diggers movement.

Diggers, meaning 'diggers', are people fond of exploring man-made underground structures, although this was also the name given to members of the poor peasantry during the English Revolution who fought against private ownership of land in the mid-17th century.

Digging, i.e. the activity of exploring the underground structures of cities, emerged as a branch of speleology at the end of the 19th and beginning of the 20th centuries. The first diggers were archaeologists, excavating forgotten dungeons for the purpose of their historical investigation. Modern diggers are, of course, nothing to do with archaeology. They are drawn to dungeons by an entirely different passion, which can be explained in terms of their acquisition of esoteric knowledge and the application of occult techniques.

Religious studies help us better discern Diggerism from a synthesis of mythological knowledge with scientific, religious, and intuitive approaches to the study of the characteristics of the Russian Diggers movement. In this paper I will be interested in the esoteric and occult sides of diggerism. For a long time the terms 'esotericism' and 'occultism' were used interchangeably, but today they have been separated by understanding esotericism as theoretical constructions and occultism as astrological, magical, alchemical and other practices involving secret or hidden forces of nature or the cosmos, which cannot be measured and understood by modern science.

1.Why do diggers need esoteric knowledge?

In the system of esoteric knowledge there is a particular classification. For example, alchemy dealing with obtaining gold, composing preparations and potions, immortality pills - is called external alchemy; and transmutation of the spirit, achieving absolute health or even immortality - is called internal alchemy. Perhaps the transmutation of one's own spirit is the most attractive aspect of digging.

In J.W. Lloyd's diggers' board book, Etidorpa or the End of the Earth. The Strange Story of a Mysterious Being' in his description of his descent into a deep underground cave back in the nineteenth century there are these words: 'It seemed to me that my endurance to bear fatigue increased to an astonishing degree... My companion replied that the cave atmosphere has an inherent animating power which neutralises fatigue, or - as he said - 'there is an inherent organic energy emanating from an active gaseous substance belonging to the air of the cave at this depth. It sustains vitality through distribution directly to its preservation, taking the place of food and drink"... "You do not understand, and how ordinary air sustains the mind and animates the muscles, and at the same time is carried away from the muscles and all other tissues. There are facts that are not satisfactorily explained by scientific statements, this includes oxygen enrichment of the blood. As we descend underground we will find an increase of vitality in the atmosphere of the caves." [*Lloyd, 2009, pp. 74-75*].

Deep dungeons draw Diggers to test their mettle, to make new discoveries and even to meet unknown civilisations.

In 1976, an experiment was conducted in Czechoslovakia on soldiers who were sent to the Krkšonė cave. The test squad had to live in the cave for 5 months. As long as there was communication with them, they reported that someone was talking to them from underground. On day 173 of the experiment, the communication wires broke. When rescuers arrived at the cave to the site of the experiment, they found only one sergeant. He told them that the rest of the team had gone deep underground to some kind of underground city.

And this is how the events that happened to the Chinese miners Wang Hu and Lao Peng are described in the 21st century: 'During the rescue work only twelve people were able to recover their bodies. The miners Lao Peng and his partner Wang Hu are trapped behind a wall of collapsed rock that is too dangerous to remove. Five years have passed since then, when suddenly, in 2008, Wang Hu, who everyone thought was dead, returned home.

The law enforcement authorities were interested because it appeared that the relatives were illegally receiving financial compensation for the miner's death. A reasonable question arose: how had Wang Hu survived and why had he not made himself known for so long?

He replied that he was prepared to compensate him for all the payments made. Wang Hu attributed his absence to the fact that he had lived in the depths of the earth for five years among the powerful Khon. After such a statement, the former miner was sent to a hospital for an examination.

After extensive and thorough examinations, the doctors concluded that their unusual patient was perfectly healthy, especially in body. There was not even the slightest sign of anthracnose, a lung disease common to almost every miner. Even more surprising was that the man had all 32 teeth, when a few years earlier he had only 25. At the age of forty, Wang Hu had the body of a 25-year-old man.

The disaster cut Wang Hu and his partner off from the surface and their comrades. The miners had an ample supply of water, but hardly any food. They waited for help for twenty-four hours before deciding to seek their own rescue. However, all the underground passages led to the depths and the men had to follow them there.

The miners were unexpectedly attacked by some low people. They did not harm the newcomers, but rather fed them and led them even lower down to where the kingdom of the Cthoneses was.

How deep the Chinese and their guides descended could only be guessed at. According to Wang Hu, the depth was about 15 kilometres. Contrary to popular theories, the temperature was tolerable and the air was clean. It was also quite bright, as the interior of the earth has a system of special lenses, up to 3,000 paces across and more than 300 meters high.

The Chents used to live in huge caves. For example, almost a thousand people lived in one of them. The Chentong language, though not at all similar to Chinese, was easy to learn, and the captives soon learned to communicate well with their surroundings. What transpired, however, was that the Chinese did not consider them captives. They sincerely believed that living on the surface was a great misfortune, and mistook the two men for fugitives seeking a way to a better world. Indeed, in the realm of the Chents no one knew hunger or disease.

Wang Hu said that the inhabitants of the dungeon fed on a special edible mould that grew in abundance in the caves. It had a peculiar and pleasant taste and was very healthy.

The Chinese quickly felt a rush of physical strength, in particular both had their teeth changed. It is not unusual for the Chinese to change their teeth many times over the course of their lives, and rarely do they live to be 200 years old. The dwellers of the dungeon do not like luxuries and content themselves with the bare minimum, but they treat them carefully and carefully. The rule of the Cthons is monarchical." [*Tolmachev, 2021, pp. 48-49*]

Contemporary diggerism is a youth subculture. In Moscow, diggers offer journeys and excursions through quarries and caves, along underground rivers, and the dungeons of old monasteries and fortresses. However, Diggers need their own mythology, legends and even a kind of quasi-religion. Therefore ideas arise about the emergence of digger heroes, capable of revealing the ancient secrets of the Kremlin, the secrets of the demolished Sukharev Tower of the blacksmith J. Bruce, the secrets of underground civilizations under cities, the mysteries of the unknown underground animal world, the secrets of underground communications, including Metro-2, the military underground secrets of the Third Reich and the Soviet empire.

All this is supported by the old rule about the sweet forbidden fruit. After all, punishment must follow for touching a secret. Thus, according to part 2 of article 20.17 of the Administrative Offences Code of the Russian Federation: unauthorized entry into an underground or underwater facility which is protected in accordance with the Russian legislation is punished with an administrative fine from 75 thousand to 200 thousand rubles; and according to article 215.4 of the Criminal Code of the Russian Federation "illegal entry into a protected facility" is punished with up to 4 years of imprisonment. It is these obstacles that further fuel the interest of young people in joining the world of diggerism - the world of underground adventures.

A teenager who entered the digger environment in the 1990s was introduced to the underground mythology, philosophy and poetry of Vadim Mikhailov, the founder and propagandist of diggerism. Anyone wishing to become a digger had to be well versed in above-ground and underground cartography, local history, history, and have skills in rescue and other work normally done by Ministry of Emergency Situations officials.

Modern diggers began to accept esoteric teachings because of the impossibility of scientific explanations of some phenomena they observe underground (for example, the emergence of underground "vortices" and "portals"), and because esoterism in modernity becomes one of the methodological principles of rethinking previously obtained scientific knowledge, as well as a useful source of new knowledge about the unity of materialistic and spiritual cognition of nature and man. F.R. Hantseverov reflects on scientific cognition of natural phenomena: "It is known, that the classical natural-scientific knowledge developed, though quite powerful toolkit, but suitable for scientific study and interpretation only of 'classical phenomena' of physical world. Outside it was the entire field of unrecognised, so-called paranormal phenomena.

Therefore world parapsychology as a whole, including astrology, ufology, biolocation, and other directions, is now busy creating a conceptual framework for their research. And this activity of searching for a methodological and theoretical platform and its introduction into practice has, unlike in the past, a significant impact on the effectiveness of ongoing research in these non-traditional fields". [*Hantseverov, 1999, p. 23*]

All esoteric knowledge is built on the postulate of similarity of microcosm and macrocosm, and therefore the influence of man on nature and nature on man is possible. For example, diggers have the notion that as a result of the interaction of states of the primary elements in the special conditions of the dungeons it is possible to carry out the transmutation of the human spirit.

2.Leaders of contemporary Russian diggers.

Here is what the biography of the leader of the Digger movement says: "Vadim Vyacheslavovich Mikhailov is the founder and leader of the international and Russian Diggers movement, "DPA" - Diggers of the Planet Underground; founder and leader of the independent unit Diggerspass; founder and president of the non-profit partnership Center for Underground Research "Diggers of the Planet Underground"; founder of the philosophy of "Inner World" and "Depth Basis" as the foundation and concentrator of life;

founder of the School of Survival in Underground and Other Megapolis Conditions, and Digger School; author and TV presenter of the educational project and historical-research, expeditionary-adventure series "Underground Odyssey". <...>

He is generally acknowledged in the world media as a "true underground legend", "an iconic figure of the underground world of the planet", a hero-observer...; a "monitoring man" who has prevented all natural and man-made disasters worldwide, and especially in Russia, working on the consequences of all terrorist attacks, collapses and failures... he has the rare, unique and perhaps the only ... gift of anticipating and anticipating disasters. <...>

Dedicated diggers personally by Vadim Mikhailov are Ilona Bronevitskaya - daughter of Edita Pieha, Renata Litvinova, Andrey Nikolaev, Nikolay Nikolaev, Roman Markov, Max Pokrovsky, Vladimir Molchanov, Anelya Merkulova, Arina Sharapova, Anastasia Chernobrovina, Roman Viktyuk, Natalia Levitskaya, Andrey Makarevich, Valerian Viktorov. <...>

He is the founder, director and collector of his own unique, as-yet-unclassified 'digger museum' of artefacts, history, archaeology and technology, fortification and polytechnics, 'objects' of science.

Poet, author of over 2,000 poems and songs, singer-songwriter. Creator of the "true underground" subculture...

Perfect autodidact self-education in the fields of geology, geophysics, biology, medicine and geomechanical theories, karstology, hydrology and hydrogeology, management, urban rescue and recovery, philosophy, psychology, fire science, mining, political science and journalism;

Graphic artist, clay and ceramic sculptor, reminiscence artist, eccentric, creative artist...". [*Mikhailov, 2009, pp. 1-6*]

3.Society and Diggers - points of contact.

The public benefit of diggers is quite high, as they warn about possible failures in cities, dangerous construction projects, the state of underground utilities and possible accidents on them. Here are some publications in Moscow newspapers: "All over Moscow, buildings are being built exceeding the existing standards by their number of storeys," explained Vadim Mikhailov, head of the Centre for Underground Research. - This has already led to many problems. The houses press so hard on the ground that they make it move and displace underground water. As a result, there are sinkholes, like the one that happened in 2007 in Trubnaya Street. Displacement of the ground, by the way, was the reason of the gas pipeline explosion in Ozernaya Street last year. And last week construction in Europe Square near Kievsky Railway Station caused a mosaic and a fragment of stucco at Kievskaya metro station to collapse... One has to understand that nothing is static under the ground, everything is in motion... Experts have confirmed that over the last 30 years over 400 small earthquakes have been registered in a city that looks calm in terms of seismology. Serious reason to wonder about the layers of the city's underground pie. According to the leader of the digger movement, about 60 per cent of all utilities are in a state of disrepair today. Among them are the pipes into which 160 rivers and streams have been buried over the last two centuries. "The walls of the collectors and tunnels have warped over time, causing leaks. A similar situation can be observed in the Neglinnaya area, near the Zoo, on Elektrichesky Lane and at Belorussky Railway Station," said Mikhailov. - Investigating pipes in some of the rivers we've found a few active leaks, which carry sewage into them. The situation is catastrophic in Oruzheyny Lane and Sukharevskaya Square. The seemingly small gaps in these places are only 'approaches' to the large internal voids. On the Kotelnicheskaya embankment our streetlight flew 20 metres into such a cavity. As a result, the hole was simply rolled up with asphalt, that's all. In Kitay-gorod, due to construction work, the temple of Zaikonospassky Monastery tilted down. The company, doing there work, dug up 250 thousand cubic meters of earth and dug up the graves of elders. The relics of the saints lay mixed in with the bones of Soviet repressed victims." It should not be forgotten that there are many other structures built at different times beneath the soles of Muscovites. For example, underground car parks,... bomb shelters, secret Metro-2 lines, etc. "We know of more than 100 such facilities," said V. Mikhailov. - They are located under Khodynka Field, in Mnevniki, in Serebryany Bor. And they are either filled with water and need major repairs, or are used as commercial warehouses, car services or gyms...". [*Aleksandrov, 2020, p. 22*].

The easiest steps in gaining knowledge about the inner earth can be done through digger studies in the underground parts of modern and ancient settlements. For this purpose, programmes should be formulated for the priority training of diggers, erudite in scientific, religious and mythological spheres.

4. How do you study digging?

Understanding diggerism requires either becoming a digger yourself or developing a friendship with their leader. In one of my works I wrote: "I met Vadim Mikhailov (born 24 April 1965), the famous leader of the international and Russian digger movement and head of the Digger Rescue Squad, in 2008. Leaving the studio at

Mosfilm after recording another TV programme, I bumped into him in the corridor... He was standing in the corridor in a bad mood and complaining... about the lack of money for some of his next search expedition.

I boldly approached Vadim, introduced myself and said: "Vadim, I am ready to help you. I promise you in front of your mother that with my help you will not go hungry. Vadim was very surprised at that time. But from then on we became friends, and I helped him and his digger movement as much as I could. Vadim taught me the tricks of the trade, showed me amazing videos and photos of the underground world, taken by himself and his associates around the world. When I asked him about the underground structures of Moscow, he told me that his father Vyacheslav Mikhailov, who was an underground engineer and maintained the underground D-6 facility, which included the system of government military tunnels under Moscow, had led him into the underground world of Moscow. This system was referred to by many as the Metro-2. Special Metro-2 trains carried separated parts of Moscow's missile defence system.

Vadim once told a journalist in an interview about Metro-2: "D-6 is indirectly connected to the regular metro, there are several gateways to go through. This facility differs from the regular metro only in that it is more technical. There is a narrower track, but not everywhere... In the centre of Moscow, near the Ministry of Defense, near GRU of General Staff, near old high-rise buildings, D-6 branch is decorated beautifully, specially for party officials. Nobody uses these stations, they stand decorated with statues at the depth of 100-300 metres in dust and stalactites, in eternal darkness... The construction underground is going on, but it is not D-6 any more. These are special bunkers, laboratories and other premises, not for the evacuation of the authorities, but for the needs of the military and special services...

There are still no general schemes of underground structures, even the KGB did not have any. Therefore, there are schemes of fragmented farms from different organisations. Hence the chaos, when something happens underground, officials start blaming each other." [*Tolmachev, 2022, pp. 80-83*]

Talking with Vadim Mikhailov, the multilayered world of our planet, of which he wrote in "The Rose of Peace" [Andreev, 2002], gradually began to reveal itself to me. [*Andreev, 2002*], the great Russian spiritualist Daniil Andreev. Diggers perceive the ideas of multilayered and multidimensional material and spiritual world not in the abstract, but concretely and practically, encountering unexplainable phenomena underground all the time.

5.Digger philosophy of the "Inner World" - mixing Christianity with esoterism.

The philosophy of the 'Inner World' and the 'Deep Basis', according to Vadim Mikhailov, leader of the Digger Movement, is 'the foundation and concentrator of modern human life' in underground space and underground time.

The basis for this philosophy is the idea of our planet as a Hollow Earth. Classical studies of the structure of the Earth from the perspective of the Hollow Earth theory have been proposed by many researchers, such as: René Descartes in his treatise The Origin of Philosophy (1644); Edmond Halley, in 1692, who said that the Earth consists of a shell of about 500 miles (about 800 km), two inner concentric shells and a central core; Leonard Euler, who suggested that the Hollow Earth lacks many shells and defined the size of the inner sun of the planet as about 1000 km.

Ray Palmer, editor of the American magazine Amazing Stories, published a series of stories in 1945-1949 called The Shaver Mystery. These stated that Shaver claimed that in ancient times the super race had built an entire system of underground structures similar to a giant beehive. Their degenerated descendants, the Deros, still live there to this day, using fantastic machines to annoy those living on the surface of the Earth. Shaver cites "voices from nowhere" as an example of mockery. Thousands of the magazine's readers have written letters to the editor confirming that they too have heard the disturbing voices from underground.

Among the most significant works on the Hollow Earth theory, in my opinion, are the works of W. J. Emerson, The Smoky God or a Voyage into the Inner World (1908) [Emerson, 2013]. The Smoky God or a Voyage to the Inner World (1908) [*Emerson, 2013*], J.W. Lloyd's Etidorhpa or the End of the Earth. The Strange Story of a Mysterious Being" (Etidorhpa The End of Earth. The man who did it, 1895) [*Lloyd, 2009*] and the Russian military researcher Leonid Ivashov "The Tumbledown World" (2020) [*Ivashov, 2020*].

Considering the Hollow Earth Theory as a kind of scientific theory, we were able to note the main differences from traditional science.

Firstly, the methods and techniques differ from those known because they actively engage the energy-informational potential of the researcher himself, acting both as a subject and as an instrument (specialists in biolocation, in regressive hypnosis, in other parapsychological properties).

Secondly, the huge number of hypotheses for the genesis of the Earth and the different facts suggest different phenomena united by the Hollow Earth theory, with different genesis.

Thirdly, with the help of the Hollow Earth theory, explorers who had not yet understood the Earth were able to derive technological and scientific benefit from the very research into the idea of the Hollow Earth.

The physical and mathematical basis of the Hollow Earth theory is based on the fundamental statements of mathematics, non-classical physics, self-organization theory, I. Prigozhin's hierarchy of inner times, and the generalized theory of order and chaos. The provisions of catastrophe theory and bifurcation theory, developments in unified field theory, theories of electromagnetism and gravitation, nonequilibrium thermodynamics, H. Haken synergetics, quantum concepts of space and time are also widely used.

The field research of the Hollow Land includes numerous travelers' reports in their extant diaries about their visits to the inner land, such as the very interesting epistle written more than five hundred years ago by Bishop Vasilii of Novgorod and sent to Bishop Fyodor of Tver. [*Tale, 1347*] The text of the epistle was published in the First Annals of Sofia (manuscript of the late fifteenth century). It describes the story of how Russian sailors discovered in the northern seas what Bishop Basil's epistle referred to as "the entrance to paradise". Bishop Basil, in his letter to Bishop Fyodor, concludes that "they turned away from that place: they could look no further at that unspeakable light, nor listen to the joy and jubilation".

J.W. Lloyd in "Etidorpa or the Edge of the Earth" describes in detail the penetration of man accompanied by a "guide from the depths of the Earth" through the Mammoth Caves at the Kentucky/Tennessee border into the depths of the Earth: "It is possible that in a future time, when man will have emptied the dismal surface of the Earth, for one day he will be forced to do as he did on the cold planets that are now uninhabited on the outer surface, nations will pass through all these spaces on their way from the sullen outer life to the delights of the healing inner sphere. Then the hour of necessity will strike here, which will surely come with the inexorable climatic changes that will control the fate of outer terrestrial life. This ever-growing storehouse, adapted to feed mankind, will be found in an accumulated state to serve as nourishment..." [*Lloyd, 2009, pp. 86-87*].

The religious or rather quasi-religious side of the Hollow Earth theory manifests itself in connection with information coming from contact persons who have voluntarily or involuntarily come into contact with "aliens" of other inner earth worlds, and which contain certain instructions, predictions, foresight or prophecies. In such cases the human contactor himself cannot keep the information to himself, unless he has been instructed in secrecy. He is obliged to pass it on to a specific person or an unspecified circle of people at a specific time.

The analysis of the esoteric, mythological and religious sides of the Hollow Earth theory and 'Inner World' philosophy forces digger studies researchers to engage not only in attempts to find the methodology, techniques and technologies of 'aliens' from the inner Earth, but also to engage seriously in religious studies of such contacts with 'aliens'. As P. Boyer says: "...There are people - not many of them - who do represent aliens in the same way as gods and spirits. In some cults, the knowledge and desires of aliens strongly influence the way of life. Actions, lifestyles, ways of thinking - there is a sense of looking back at aliens from other worlds everywhere." [*Boyer, 2017, p. 226-227*].

The religious and mythological side of Diggerism and the Hollow Earth are firmly connected to the mythology and religion of the Living Earth, and quickly find their way to the hearts of Diggers themselves and many others. Dugin A. G. Dugin wrote: "Popular religion in the spirit of twilight consciousness and 'Dionysian' dialectics does not deny this distinction, but it does not affirm it either. God, of course, is superior to man, but not to the extent that there is an abyss between them. Popular faith accentuates the superiority of God only together with his intimacy. Hence the stories of how God (sometimes with his companions) walked the earth, visited peasants' houses, healed, raised from the dead and performed miracles... God is not beyond the border, or rather, He is, but this border is porous, transparent, like the border between life and death, between reality and Navia, between people and the dead. Therefore, God is not exclusive, but inclusive; he includes the world, not excludes it... And this is where the mystical side of Christianity comes to the fore: the notion of Jesus Christ as both God and Man, of his overcoming death by death, of his descent into hell and resurrection, of his dwelling among men and the transformation of his sacred flesh, of the infinite pity and kindness of the Mother of God, suffering even for those who are quite rightly tormented in hell, of miracles, of healings and the unexpected intercession of higher powers, of the appearances of angels, saints and icons, of the conversion of sinners, despised tax collectors and robbers (the Apostle Matthew, Zacchaeus, Mary Magdalene, Mary of Egypt, the Wise Robber, the Barbarian of Lucas, Moses of Murine, etc.).д.).

This part is present in the full-fledged Christian doctrine, but the people choose this side, which corresponds to their deepest faith - the religion of (Russian) Earth, which in secret is Heaven." [Dugin, 2019, p. 289-290].

Among Moscow's Diggers, according to their leader, almost all are Orthodox Christians. There is no place for non-believing atheists underground, says Mikhailov. They never go underground without collective and individual prayers to their patrons and protectors - Archangel Michael and St. Nicholas the Wonderworker. Vadim Mikhailov told me that in critical moments underground, when a digger's life hangs in the balance, only a loud prayer appeal to Archangel Michael has saved them more than once.

The Diggers are convinced that the Hollow Earth Theory, together with the philosophy of the "Inner World", is a science, a myth, an emerging religious cult, esoteric knowledge, as well as a break through the veils of any religious cult to the Creator, to the Cosmos, to the living planet Earth, to the human spirit and souls of all living beings, and most importantly - one of the ways to human self-organisation in the living world.

The self-organisation of man and the entire living world destroys the artificial world, because it is only possible in the living world by receiving living creative energy from "nowhere" (as atheist philosophers explain), from resonance (as physicists explain), from the divine grace of the Holy Spirit (as theologians explain).

The analysis of the religious and esoteric conceptions of diggers leads to the idea that esotericism and occultism as a socio-cultural and religious phenomenon represent a set of instructions for digger's behavior in different life situations in the underworld. The task of the various esoteric concepts is similar to that of the religious

(Christian) and mythological concepts - to bring order to society, to an order of a higher level than that currently experienced by man. In the language of modern physics, in all known periods of life of human society, the entropy of human society grows, i.e. the fall of the vital order and the increase of chaos. Science, religion, mythology, esoterics - all of them give man tools to order his life, reduce entropy and increase structural order of human society.

List of references:

1.Aleksandrov G. Payment for failure // Argumenty i Fakty, 2020, No. 4. - c. 22.

2.Andreev D.L. The Rose of the World / D.L. Andreev - M.: Mir Uraniya, 2002. - 608 c. ISBN 5-900191-25-7.

3.Boyer P. Explaining Religion: The Nature of Religious Thinking / translated from French by M. Desiatova - M.: Alpina Conflict, 2017.

4.Dugin, A.G. Noomachia: War of the Mind. Russian Logos I. The Kingdom of Earth, The Structure of Russian Identity / A.G. Dugin - Moscow: Academic Project, 2019. - 461 c. - ISBN 978-5-8291-2384-0.

5.Ivashov L. Overturned world / Leonid Ivashov - M.: Publishing house "Argumenty Nedeli" JSC, 2020. - 384 c. ISBN 978-5-6043544-1-4.

6.The Emerald Tablet / Text, translation and comments by K. Bogutsky // Hermes Trismegistus and the Hermetic tradition of the West. - Kiev-M., 1998. ISBN 966-7068-06-4.

7.Lloyd J.W. Etidorhpa or the End of the Earth. The strange story of a mysterious creature (Etidorhpa The End of Earth. The man who did it, 1895) / J. W. Lloyd / translated from English by N. Bugaenko - Toronto, 2009. - 244 c. - ill. - (http://www.myshambhala.com).

8.The Book of Magicians / comp. V. Rokhmistrova - SPb.: Amfora, TID Amfora. 2009. - 314 c. ISBN 978-5-367-01024-4.

9.Mikhailov V. V. A brief closed general internal brief. 2009. - 8 c.

10.Narrative of the Bishop of Novgorod - (http://nlo-mir.ru/paramir/5stranyrasskaznovgorodskogo-episkopa.html) Material taken from: The Epistle of Basil, Archbishop of Novgorod, to Feodor, Bishop of Tver, on the earthly paradise, under 1347 (vv. 422-428).

11. Tolmachev A. V. Hollow Earth: Science + Religion + Myth. Part 1. / A. V. Tolmachev - Chisinau, Moldova - EU: LAP Lambert Academic Publishing, 2021, - 148 p. ISBN 978-620-4-73180-3.

12. Tolmachev A. V. Hollow Earth: Science + Religion + Myth. Part 2. / A. V. Tolmachev - Chisinau, Moldova - EU: LAP Lambert Academic Publishing, 2022, - 135 p. ISBN 978-620-0-09410-0.

13.Hantseverov F.R. Eniology: miracles without mysticism. Book of scientific versions / F.R. Hantseverov - M.: International Academy of Energy and Information Sciences. ASM, 1999. - 445 c. ISBN 5-900576-08-6.

14.Hall Manley P. The Secret Teachings: An Encyclopaedic Statement of Hermetic, Kabbalistic and Rosencreutzian Symbolic Philosophy / Manley P. Hall / translated from English by V.V. Tselischeva. - M.: KoLibri, Azbuka-Attikus, 2019. - 960 p.: ill. ISBN 978-5-389-13333-4.

15. Emerson, W. J. J. The Smoky God or a Voyage to the Inner World, 1908 / W. J. Emerson / translated by E. Lavretskaya, 2013. J. Emerson / translated from English by E. Lavretskaya, 2013. - www.tempelvril.org.

3. *A. V. Tolmachev* **Scientific studies of the Hollow Earth Theory.**

(article for the Round Table "The Theory of Occultation: Meaning, Applications, Perspectives", Moscow, AIEM, 2022, 24 May)

Introduction.

The object of the research in this article is the planet Earth as part of the spiritual and practical life of modern man, through which man tries to answer questions about the genesis of the Earth and about the good or evil that enters into human life with the advent of the Hollow Earth theory.

The subject is part of the contemporary Hollow Earth theory, aimed at the formation of mythological concepts and the emergence of a quasi-religious cult in the Diggers' movement.

The aim of the study is to try to answer questions about the influence of the modern Hollow Earth hypothesis on the emergence of quasi-religious cults, as well as about the possibility of adapting ancient myths (cosmological and others) or constructing new myths to create conditions for peaceful natural-science and religious-intuitive research of the planet genesis from the perspective of the Hollow Earth theory and debunking of quasi-religious cults.

In order to realise the aim of the study, the following objectives are being pursued:

(a) Consider the Hollow Earth theory as a scientific, technical, socio-cultural and religious phenomenon;

b) consider the Hollow Earth theory as a natural science tool for gaining knowledge about the planet;

c) consider the Hollow Earth theory as a religious and mythological tool for gaining knowledge about the planet;

d) Consider the Hollow Earth theory as a new synthesised tool for knowing the cosmos, the planet and man, incorporating scientific, religious, mythological and intuitive cognition.

1.History of scientific research into the Hollow Earth theory.

The classical scientific study of the structure of the Earth from the perspective of the Hollow Earth theory has been proposed by many researchers, such as: René Descartes in his treatise The Origin of Philosophy (1644), Edmond Halley in 1692, who said that the Earth consists of shells of about 500 miles (about 800 km), two inner concentric shells and a central core with diameters corresponding to Venus, Mars and Mercury. The shells are separated by atmospheres and each shell has its own magnetic poles. The spheres rotate at different speeds. Halley proposed this model as an explanation for the anomalous behaviour of the compass. He imagined the inner atmosphere to be luminous (and probably inhabited) and suggested that the leakage of the inner luminous atmosphere was the cause of the northern lights.

Leonard Euler, according to De Kamp and Ley (in "Lands Beyond"), suggested that the Hollow Earth lacks many shells and defined the size of the inner sun as about 620 miles (about 1000 km). John Leslie, according to the same De Kamp and Ley, suggested the presence of two suns in the Hollow Earth: Pluto and Proserpine. In Elements of Natural Philosophy (1829), John Leslie outlined his own theory of the Hollow Earth.

Le Clerc Milford reported that on an exploratory expedition with Indians near Red River in 1781, he learned that the ancestors of the Creeks had come to the surface of the Earth in ancient times from caves. Milford reported that the caves he was able to see "could easily accommodate 15-20 thousand families".

In 1818, John Cleaves Simms, Jr. suggested that the Earth consisted of a hollow shell 800 miles (about 1,300 km) thick, with holes at the poles about 1,400 miles (about 2,300 km) in diameter. On 15 April 1818 he sent a letter to congressmen, scientists and university presidents inviting them to help him on an expedition to prove the Hollow Earth theory. He wrote: "To all the world. I declare that the Earth is hollow and inhabited from within. It consists of several solid concentric spheres, one inside the other, and has openings at the poles from 12 to 16 degrees. I undertake to prove this statement true and am willing to explore the interior of the Earth if I am assisted in this enterprise. Cleve Simms, former Captain in the Infantry. He later put his ideas about Hollow Earth into a book in 1828. After Simms' death in 1829, his son continued his father's work and put forward the idea that within the Hollow Earth lived the ten lost tribes of Israel.

McBride in 1826 wrote the book "Simms's Theory of Concentric Spheres". Jeremiah Reynolds in 1827 published a paper "Notes on Simms's theory published in the Quarterly Review". Professor W.F. Lyons in 1868 published The Hollow Ball, elaborating on the Hollow Earth theory. Later Amerikus Simms published his book "Simms Concentric Sphere Theory".

William Reed published The Pole Phantom in 1906, developing the idea of a Hollow Earth without inner spheres or inner suns. In 1913, Marshall Gardner wrote Journey Into the Deep Earth, in which he placed an inner sun inside the Hollow Earth. Gardner created a working model of the Hollow Earth and patented it.

The American electrophysicist Cyrus Tiede, studying myths and legends, came to the conclusion in 1864 that modern humans did not live on the outer, but on the inner surface of the Earth in the underworld. At the same time, Teed founded the occult doctrine of Koreshanism (or Koreshism).

The German aviator Bender, after encountering the writings of Cyrus Tiede in a French prisoner of war camp after World War I, published in various issues of The Flaming Sword, became concerned with Corehism and suggested that the planet was a huge bubble located in a rock, where the air layer occupied 60 kilometres. This was followed by a rarefied atmosphere reaching to the very core of the absolute void, where a mass of rounded "primordial matter" lodged, around which the tiny moon and sun and small luminous particles in the form of galaxies, stars and planets orbit. The change of day and night on the concavities occurs when the sun sets behind the mass. In 1942, Bender took part in an expedition to the island of Rügen, led by Heinz Fischer, to test the hypothesis of modern human life on a concave surface inside the Earth using radar. After the failure of the expedition, Bender died in a German concentration camp.

Bender's ideas were developed by Liu Cixin in his work of fiction, The Wandering Earth (2013)[1].

Raymond Bernard in his book The Hollow Earth (1969) not only developed the Hollow Earth theory but also suggested that UFOs appear from the inside of the Earth. Bernard himself disappeared into the caves of South America in the late 1960s. The full story of Bernard became known after the publication of Walter

---

1 Liu Cixin Wandering Earth [Text] / Liu Cixin / translated from English by N. Ibragimova. - Moscow: Eksmo, 2021. - 480 c. ISBN 978-5-04-117996-0.

Kafton-Minkel's book Underworlds: 100,000 Years of Dragons, Dwarves, the Dead, Vanished Races and UFOs in the Earth's Interior (1989).

Ray Palmer, as editor of the American magazine Amazing Stories, published a series of stories from 1945-1949 called The Shaver Mystery. These stated that Shaver claimed that in ancient times the super race had built an entire system of underground structures similar to a giant beehive. Their degenerated descendants, the Deros, still live there to this day, using fantastic machines to annoy those living on the surface of the Earth. Shaver cites "voices from nowhere" as an example of mockery. Thousands of readers of the magazine have written letters to the editor confirming that they too have heard intimidating voices from underground.

In addition to researchers, many writers have used the Hollow Earth model: E. A. Poe's A Tale of the Adventures of Arthur Gordon Pym (1838), Jules Verne's Journey to the Centre of the Earth (1864), A. Merritt's Moonwaters (1918), V. A. Obruchev's Plutonium (1924), and A. and B. Strugatsky's Inhabited Island (1969). Strugatsky "The Inhabited Island" (1969), K. Bulychev "The Purple Ball" (1982), several German writers including Peter Bender, Johannes Lang, Karl Neupert, Fritz Braun and others have published works in defence of the Hollow Earth theory (Hohlweltlehre).

Among the most significant works for the study of the Hollow Earth theory in my opinion are: W. J. Emerson's The Smoky God or a Voyage into the Inner World (1908). The Smoky God or a Voyage to the Inner World (1908)[2] , J.W. Lloyd's Etidorhpa or the End of the Earth. The Strange Story of a Mysterious Being (Etidorhpa The End

---

2 Emerson W. J. J. The Smoky God or a Voyage to the Inner World, 1908 / W. J. Emerson / translated by E. Lavretskaya, 2013. J. Emerson / translated from English by E. Lavretskaya, 2013. - www.tempelvril.org.

of Earth. The man who did it, 1895)[3] , and Russian military researcher Leonid Ivashov's The Tilted World (2020)[4] .

Such researchers as V. G. Azhazha[5] , E. Daniken[6] , V. P. Kaznacheev[7] , V. A. Chernoborov[8] , J. Vallée[9] and others have indirectly referred to the Hollow Earth theory, without fully supporting it.

In today's Russia, researchers and proponents of the Hollow Earth theory operate without uniform coordination. Some of the research tasks are carried out by state and military special institutes, some by scientists from different branches of science privately funded by business, and some by dilettantes who organise research at their own risk without access to state and special archives.

The religious or rather quasi-religious side of the Hollow Earth theory manifests itself in connection with information coming from contact persons who have voluntarily or involuntarily come into contact with "aliens" of other inner earth worlds, and which contain certain instructions, predictions, foresight or prophecies. In such cases the human contactor himself cannot keep the information to himself, unless he has been instructed in secrecy. He is obliged to

---

3 Lloyd J.W. Etidorhpa or the End of the Earth. The strange story of a mysterious creature (Etidorhpa The End of Earth. The man who did it, 1895) / J. W. Lloyd / translated from English by N. Bugaenko - Toronto, 2009. - 244 c. - ill. - (http://www.myshambhala.com).
4 Ivashov L. Overturned world [Text] / Leonid Ivashov - M.: Publishing house "Argumenty Nedeli" JSC, 2020. - 384 c. ISBN 978-5-6043544-1-4
5 Azhazha V. G. The Ufological Mystery. Book one. Euphoria. [Text] / V.G. Azhazha - M.: AIF-Print, 2002. - 320 c. (series "Edge of our world"). - ISBN 5-94736-001-2.
6 Daniken E. The Stone Age was different... [Text] / Erich von Daniken / translated from German. - Moscow: Eksmo Publisher. 2003. - 288 p., ill. IBSN 5-699-03983-X.
7 Kaznacheev V. P. P. Cosmogony of the Planet and the Gaia Programme. [Kaznacheev V.P. - Novosibirsk: Nauka, 1997.
8 Chernobrov V. A. Mystery of time [Text] / V. Chernobrov - M.: Olimp; LLC Firma "AST Publisher", 1999. - 512 p., ill. (Encyclopedia of mysterious and unknown) - ISBN 5-7390-0872-7.
9 Vallee J. F. UFO Chronicles of the Soviet Union: A Cosmic Samizdat. New York: Balantine Boocks, 1992.

pass it on to a specific person or an unspecified circle of people at a specific time.

Active interest in the Hollow Earth theory has recently been linked to the mass nature of UFO sightings, as some contacts claim that aliens who make contact with them are reporting their presence on the inner side of our planet. "Contactors and ufology researchers are clearly divided into several groups that report different origins for UFOs and the aliens themselves. One group claims that in the present and past UFO objects and aliens have come from outer space: from other planets, star systems, galaxies. Another group of contactors and ufology researchers report aliens arriving from deep within our planet: from the thickness of the Earth's crust or from the interior of the hollow Earth. A third group of contactors and researchers report aliens arriving from other spatial or temporal dimensions: from parallel universes; from the fourth or higher quasi-space; from other time (up to and including time-machine travel)".[10]

The smallest group of contactors and ufology researchers[11] report information about beings (the vast majority of people are completely similar to us) arriving in our world from future time or from parallel worlds. Many predictions of events in human civilisation have been received just from aliens arriving from future time.

---

10 Tolmachev A. V. Logos of State vs Logos of People : collection of scientific articles [Text] / A. V. Tolmachev - Riga, Latvia, EU: LAP Lambert Academic Publishing, 2021, - 86 p. - ISBN 978-620-3-30543-2
11 Chernobrov V. A. Mystery of time [Text] / V. Chernobrov - M.: Olimp; LLC Firma "AST Publisher", 1999. - 512 p., ill. (Encyclopedia of mysterious and unknown) - ISBN 5-7390-0872-7.

Most interesting in my view is the third group of contactors and ufology researchers[12] reporting on aliens from our own planet. This line of research has been particularly active in the last 30 years. The explanation is quite simple. If all researchers and various government agencies (police, military, security services, 911 and EMERCOM) record up to half a million reports of contacts with UFOs and aliens every year, it is unlikely that so many interplanetary flights are taking place. It is more likely that it is our co-planners living near us.

2.Field Studies in Hollow Earth Theory.

In my book Hollow Earth: Science + Religion + Myth. Part I."[13] I wrote: "Field studies can include numerous reports by travellers in their surviving diaries of visits to the inner Earth.

y. Willis George Emerson (28.03.1856 - 10.12.1918), American writer, Chicago newspaperman, lawyer, politician, promoter, founder of the North American Copper Company and the town of Encampment in Wyoming published a book with diary entries and maps of Olaf Jansen, who travelled with his father to the inner earth and lived there for almost two years.

Here are some excerpts from his publication.

"One of the most able works of recent years is Paradise Found, or The Cradle of Man in the North Pole, by William F. Warren. In his thoroughly finished volume, Mr Warren almost bumps his finger at the real truth, but misses, apparently, only a little, if the old Scandinavian's discovery is correct. Dr Orville

12 Azhazha V. G. The Ufological Mystery. Book Three. Creation of the world: the eighth day. [Text] / V.G. Azhazha - M.: "AIF-Print", 2002. - 332 c. (series "Facets of our world"). - ISBN 5-94736-003-9
13 Tolmachev A. V. Hollow Earth: science + religion + myth. Part 1. [Text] / A. V. Tolmachev - Chisinau, Moldova - EU: LAP Lambert Academic Publishing, 2021, - 148 p. ISBN 978-620-4-73180-3.

Livingston Leech, a scientist, in a recent article, says: "The probabilities of a world within the Earth first presented themselves to my attention when I picked up a gyode on the shores of the Great Lakes. The jode is a spherical and obviously solid rock, but when it is broken, it is seen to be hollow and covered with crystals. The Earth is only a large form of the jode, and the law that created the jode with its hollow form undoubtedly moulded the Earth in the same way." In introducing the subject of this almost unbelievable story, as told by Olof Jansen, and accompanied by a manuscript, maps and rough drawings entrusted to me, a suitable introduction is found in the following quote: "In the beginning God created the heavens and the earth, and the earth was without form and empty." And also, "God created man in his own likeness". Therefore, even in the material material, man must be Godlike, because he is created in the likeness of the Father. Man builds a house for himself and his family. Entrances and porches are all outside, and secondary. The building, really built for comfort, is on the inside. Olaf Jansen makes a terrific announcement through me, a humble tool, that in a similar fashion, God created the earth for the 'inside' - that is, for its lands, seas, rivers, mountains, forests and valleys, and for its other internal comforts, while the outside of the earth is simply a veranda, an entranceway, where things grow similar but sparse, like lichen on the mountain side, clinging resolutely to bare existence. Take an eggshell, and from each end remove a piece as large as the end of this pencil. Remove its contents and then you have a fine representation of Olaf Jansen's land. The distance from the inner surface to the outer surface, according to him, is approximately three hundred miles (482.8032 km?). The centre of gravity is not at the centre of the earth, but at the centre of the shell or crust; therefore, if the crust of the earth or crust is three hundred miles thick, the centre of gravity is one hundred and fifty miles below the surface. In their watch logs, Arctic explorers tell us about the inclination of the compass needle as the ship approaches areas of farthest known north. In reality, they are sailing along a curve; at the edge of the shell, where gravity increases exponentially, and while the electric current appears to be carried off into space towards the ghostly idea of the North Pole, all the same electric current descends again and continues its course southwards along the inner surface of the Earth's crust. In an appendix to his work Captain Sabine makes an account of experiments to determine the acceleration of the pendulum at different latitudes. This seems to have followed from the combined work of Piri and Sabine. He says: "The accidental discovery that the pendulum, being removed from Paris to the equator increased its time of oscillation, gave a first step to our latest findings that the polar axis of the globe is less than the equatorial; that the force of gravity in the earth's surface increases progressively from the equator to the poles." According to Olaf Jansen, our outer world was created solely for the 'inner' world, where the four great rivers - Euphrates, Pisan, Gihon and Hiddekel... On top of a high mountain, near the source of these four rivers, Olaf Jansen claims to have discovered the long-lost 'Garden of Paradise', 'the true navel of the Earth', and has spent over two years studying and exploring in this amazing 'inner' land, abundant, with enormous plants and gigantic animals; a land where people have lived for centuries, like Methuselah and other biblical characters, an area where one quarter of the "inner" surface is land and three quarters water; where there are great oceans and many rivers and lakes; where cities are superb in construction and splendour; where modes of transportation are as far from ours as we with our achievements before the inhabitants of "darkest Africa". The distance directly through space from the inner surface to the inner surface is about six hundred miles less than the recognised diameter of the earth. At the centre of this vast vacuum is the seat of electricity - a giant ball of dim red fire - not strikingly brilliant, but surrounded by a white, temperate, bright cloud, emitting uniform heat, and remaining in its place in the centre of this inner world by the unchanging law of gravity. This electric cloud is known to people 'inside' as the abode of the 'Smoky God'."[14]

J.W. Lloyd's book, Etidorpa or the Edge of the Earth. The Strange Story of a Mysterious Creature' is one of the amazing and detailed diaries of an inland traveller. Here is a small excerpt from it: "We have been continually sinking under the earth, and are now ten miles or more below ocean level... You enter the zone of the inner light of the earth, we are at its surface, the upper edge of the zone... Can philosophers, engage in more than simple speculation about what they have not experienced, if they have no data on which to make calculations? Name me a student of science who has reached this depth of the earth, or a person who has been told these facts?"[15]

As for me personally, I decided to follow the path described by travellers into the depths of the planet. However, as I pointed out in my book "Hollow Earth: Science + Religion + Myth. Part 2." "Having failed to get the desired results from the expedition to Epomeo Volcano and from the first Arctic expedition, I tried to

<hr>

14   Emerson W. J. J. The Smoky God, or a Journey into the Inner World (The Smoky God, 1908) / W. J. Emerson. J. Emerson / translated from English by E. Lavretskaya, 2013. - www.tempelvril.org - p.4-5.
15 Lloyd J.W. Etidorhpa or the End of the Earth. The strange story of a mysterious creature (Etidorhpa The End of Earth. The man who did it, 1895) / J. W. Lloyd / translated from English by N. Bugaenko - Toronto, 2009. - 244 c. - ill. - (http://www.myshambhala.com) - p. 76.

prepare a new expedition deep into the Earth through the Mammoth Caves in the USA.

From the detailed description of the passage deep into the Earth in J.W. Lloyd's book, I understood not only the clear geographical coordinates of the passage at the Tennessee-Kentucky border, but also the conditions under which the descent was possible at all.

First, either a man who has broken away from all his life and attachments on the surface of the Earth can go there, or a woman with additional restrictions - either a virgin or having passed the stage of menopause. This strange restriction for women would seem to make no common sense. But only until one finds evidence of abduction of women of child-bearing age by subterranean inhabitants.

Secondly, you must not take any foodstuffs with you on your underground journey, nor any special devices such as shovels, knives, ropes, etc. All these gadgets are very annoying for the inhabitants in the thickness of the earth's crust. And food is plentiful there in the forms of underground huge mushrooms and lichens. This has also been confirmed by reports of the Chinese miner Wang Hu, who came out after living in the deep subterranean depths of the Kogon people for five years from 2008 to 2013[16].

Thirdly, instead of measuring instruments, one had to train one's own body to sense changes in temperature or gravitational gradients. Torches were not necessary either. It was clear from the book that at a depth of more than 15 km underground one could see everything, as an even milky-white light was shining through the walls of caves and tunnels. This was also claimed by the Chinese miner Wang Hu in 2013.

---

16 Two miners missing - (http://www.myshambhala.com)

Three people were selected for the expedition. The first is Vadim Mikhailov (born 1965), a famous Russian digger, explorer of underground cities. The second is Lyudmila Romanova (b. 1962), a famous Russian traveller to the hidden lands of the Russian North and Siberia, whom I call "stalker" because she was able to make contacts with the hidden inhabitants and keepers of tundra, forest and mountains, as well as to overcome peaceful obstacles of all kinds of keepers of earthly and underground secrets. The third is Irina Guildenbrandt (b.1993), a specialist in reconnaissance and special operations. I have also enlisted my son Ivan Tolmachev (born 1990), an information technology specialist and resident in San Francisco, to support the expedition.

I expected the expedition to take place in October-November 2016. The task before the expedition participants was very specific. To descend through one of the entrances to the Mammoth Caves for a fortnight to a depth of about 15 km, to detect through their own senses changes in gravity and changes in illumination, and then to exit back out within two to three weeks.

However, the expedition could not take place, as since September 2016, the US federal authorities have banned descents into the Mammoth Caves, and a member (a close friend of Lyudmila Romanova) of one such government expedition from the US reported that the Americans have banned members of underground expeditions from staying more than three months in the Mammoth Caves, forbidding the exchange of information about the discoveries. On government underground expeditions, the Americans hire specialists from all over the world, from physicists and biologists to psychics and alchemists.

Then I realised that something really serious had happened in 2015-2016 between the inhabitants of the Earth's surface, the Earth's thickness and the Earth's inner cavity. I think that, in time, everything will become clearer and I will be able to carry out what I have planned."[17]

Conclusions.

In considering the various hypotheses about the genesis of the Earth and the Hollow Earth theory as a scientific field, we have been able to note the main differences from the methods of the conventional Earth sciences.

Firstly, the research methods and techniques in Hollow Earth Theory differ from the known ones, as they actively engage the energy-informational potential of the researcher himself, acting both as a subject and an instrument (contactors, specialists in biolocation, regressive hypnosis, other parapsychological properties).

Secondly, the sheer number of hypotheses for the genesis of the Earth and the different facts suggest different phenomena united by the Hollow Earth theory, with different genesis.

Thirdly, with the help of the Hollow Earth theory, researchers who had not yet understood the Earth were able to derive technological and scientific benefits from the very research into the idea of the Hollow Earth in other branches of knowledge.

Fourthly, the analysis of new information from scientific, religious, mythological studies in terms of the Hollow Earth theory, as well as field studies and observations - makes researchers not only try to find new scientific instruments, techniques and

---

17 Tolmachev A. V. Hollow Earth: science + religion + myth. Part 2. [Text] / A. V. Tolmachev - Chisinau, Moldova - EU: LAP Lambert Academic Publishing, 2022, - 135 p. ISBN 978-620-0-09410-0. pp. 78-79.

technologies to study the inner Earth, but also seriously engage in research on new sources of information not related to traditional ones, such as information from contacts with other civilisations.

Fifth, personal experience has shown that not always well-prepared expeditions following the footsteps of earlier travellers into the depths of the Earth can be absolutely successful. However, it is necessary to head for new field studies of the planet, relying not only on scientific technical instruments, but also to prepare your spirit and your body to receive the maximum informational effect from your own senses, including the gravitational sense.

Sixthly, the easiest steps in gaining knowledge of the inner earth can be done through digger studies in the underground parts of modern and ancient settlements. For this purpose, it is necessary to formulate programmes for the priority training of diggers, erudite in scientific, religious and mythological spheres.

Seventh, the most promising areas of research on our planet from the perspective of the Hollow Earth Theory are as follows: continuing scientific research into the planet's magnetic and gravitational fields; scientific research into the inner Earth using seismic waves as well as modern "neutrino telescopes"; religious studies of cosmological texts of different peoples; scientific and religious studies of modern contactors with other civilisations and inhabitants of different layers of the Earth.

List of references:

1. Azhazha V.G. Ufological Mystery. Book One. Euphoria. [Text] / V.G. Azhazha - M.: AIF-Print, 2002. - 320 c. (series "Edge of our world"). - ISBN 5-94736-001-2.

2. Daniken E. Stone Age was different... [Text] / Erich von Daniken / translated from German. - Moscow: Eksmo Publisher. 2003. - 288 p., ill. IBSN 5-699-03983-X.

3.Ivashov L. Overturned world / Leonid Ivashov - M.: Publishing house "Argumenty Nedeli" JSC, 2020. - 384 c. ISBN 978-5-6043544-1-4.

4. Kaznacheev V. P. P. Cosmogony of Planet and Gaia Programme. [Text] / V.P. Kaznacheev - Novosibirsk: Nauka, 1997.

5.Lloyd J.W. Etidorhpa or the End of the Earth. The strange story of a mysterious creature (Etidorhpa The End of Earth. The man who did it, 1895) / J. W. Lloyd / translated from English by N. Bugaenko - Toronto, 2009. - 244 c. - ill. - (http://www.myshambhala.com).

6. Liu Cixin Wandering Earth [Text] / Liu Cixin / translated from English by N. Ibragimova. - Moscow: Eksmo, 2021. - 480 c. ISBN 978-5-04-117996-0.

7.Missing two miners- (http://www.myshambhala.com).

8.Tolmachev A. V. Hollow Earth: Science + Religion + Myth. Part 1. / A. V. Tolmachev - Chisinau, Moldova - EU: LAP Lambert Academic Publishing, 2021, - 148 p. ISBN 978-620-4-73180-3.

9.Tolmachev A. V. Hollow Earth: Science + Religion + Myth. Part 2. / A. V. Tolmachev - Chisinau, Moldova - EU: LAP Lambert Academic Publishing, 2022, - 135 p. ISBN 978-620-0-09410-0.

10. Chernobrov V.A. Mystery of time [Text] / V. Chernobrov - M.: Olimp; LLC Firma "AST Publisher", 1999. - 512 p., ill. (Encyclopedia of mysterious and unknown) - ISBN 5-7390-0872-7.

11. Emerson W. J. J. The Smoky God or a Voyage to the Inner World, 1908 / W. J. Emerson / translated by E. Lavretsky, 2013. J. Emerson / translated from English by E. Lavretskaya, 2013. - www.tempelvril.org.

12. Vallee J. F. UFO Chronicles of the Soviet Union: A Cosmic Samizdat. New York: Balantine Boocks, 1992.

4. *A. V. Tolmachev* **Daniel Andreev's Religious Methods of Investigating the Multidimensional Earth (Shadanakare) - a Source of Knowledge about the Deep Worlds.**

(article for XXVI Tsarskoselsky Readings, St. Petersburg, A. S. Pushkin Leningrad State University, 2022, 19-20 April)

1.A kind of religious cognition.

Д. L. Andreev distinguishes three kinds of religious cognition: 1) metahistorical; 2) transphysical; 3) ecumenical.

Д. L.Andreev writes: "Speaking about the metahistorical method of cognition, I have imperceptibly passed to the transphysical: the wanderings and meetings I have told, partly belong already to the field of transphysical cognition... Perhaps some will express surprise: why instead of the generally understood word "spiritual" I so often use the term "transphysical". But the word 'spiritual' in its strict sense legitimately refers only to God and monads. But the term "transphysical" applies to everything that has materiality, but other than ours, to all worlds existing in spaces with a different number of coordinates and in other flows of time. By transphysical (in the sense of the object of cognition) I understand the whole totality of such worlds regardless of the processes occurring there. Such processes connected with the formation of Shadanakar constitute metahistory; connected with the formation of the Universe - meta-evolution; cognition of meta-evolution is cognition of the Universe. The word "transphysics" in the sense of religious doctrine means the doctrine of the structure of Shadanakar. The objects of metahistorical cognition are related to history and culture, transphysical cognition is related to the nature of our layer and other layers of Shadanakar, and universal cognition is related to the universe. Thus, those phenomena which I have called transphysical wanderings and encounters can, depending on their content, be referred either to the metahistorical kind of cognition, or to the transphysical, or to the universal." [*Andreev, 2002, p. 70-71*].

2.Where did the cruel laws of evolution and karma of Shadanakar (mono-dimensional earth) come from?

Daniel Andreev tries to explain the cruelty of the laws of evolution and karma in the living world on Earth: "Religions of Semitic origin are characterized by the desire to place responsibility for the cruelty of the laws on the Deity. Surprisingly, there was no protest, not even an awareness of their very brutality, at least not the brutality of the laws of retribution. With an incomprehensible serenity, even the righteous of Christian meta-cultures tolerated the notion of eternal suffering of sinners. The absurdity of the eternal retribution for temporal evil did not worry their minds, and their conscience - it is not clear how - was satisfied with the idea of the eternal inviolability, i.e. the hopelessness of these laws. But that state of mind and conscience passed long ago. And it seems blasphemous to us to think that this law, as it exists, was created by divine will.

Yes, not a single hair will fall without the will of the Heavenly Father, not a single leaf on the tree will be moved. But this is not to be understood in the sense that the whole world Law in its totality is a manifestation of the Will of God, but that the formation of the free-will which the universe represents is sanctioned by God. From the existence of a multitude of free wills arose the possibility of the falling away of some of them; from their falling away arose their struggle with the forces of Light and their creation of an Anticosmos which is opposed to the Creator's Cosmos.

Ever since the emergence of living life in Enroph, Gagtungr and his packs have had their paw on the laws of that life. They have failed to change the laws of the middle layers of Shadanakar, but many species and classes of the animal kingdom and some layers of the elementals have fallen under their dominion - in whole or in part. Hence the duality of what we call nature: beauty, spirituality, harmony, friendliness on the one hand, and the general mutualism of living beings on the other. Is it not obvious that both sides are equally real? Can any man of conscience and intellect, however ardently he may love nature, dare say that her harmony covers and removes the boundless sea of suffering, which the same nature presents to the unbiased eye? And is there even a single man, who in spite of this sea of sufferings, so manifest, so undeniable, so silently deafening us by the moans and cries of the living creatures, would not occasionally experience the nature as an inexplicable, in spite of everything abiding harmony and incomparable beauty? Why is it that this fateful contradiction has not yet been understood and solved? Is it not because for more than twenty centuries the religious thought in the West has been captive to the idea of absolute omnipotence of God and consequent prejudices about the unity of Nature, and in the East the fixed philosophical monism does not give us to understand its duality? [*Andreev, 2002, p. 164-165*].

3.The deep infernal worlds of Shadanakar (mono-dimensional Earth).

Daniel Andreev says: "The first hypostasis of the Divine Trinity Gagtungr seeks to confront its first face - the Great Tormentor, the second hypostasis - the second face, which is most accurately described by the name of the Great Harlot, and the third hypostasis of the Trinity is opposed by the antipode, called Urparp:

it is the executor of the demonic plan; in a sense it may be called the principle of form: it is that side of the great demonic being which is revealed in the life of the various strata of Shadanakar as the beginning which actively remakes their givenness according to the intentions and purposes of the Tormentor, the beginning which forms. The Great Harlot - her name is Fokerma - the side of the demonic being that draws in, sucks souls and destinies into the orbit of Gagtungr. The first person, Histurg, the Great Tormentor, is the last depth of the demonic self, the bearer of the highest will, power and desire.

The image of him, as seen through the spiritual eyes of the few people who have penetrated the dark heights of Digma, his world, is immensely creepy....

There is an even higher demonic layer in Shadanakar: this is the multidimensional Shog, whose materiality is created by the great demons of the macroframeworks. Here flow powerful streams of inspirational, involuting divine forces from the depths of the universe, and no one but Gagtungr can enter this layer; the others, and this in the rarest of moments, are only able to see it from the outside. In those moments they perceive that glow of ineffable colour that blazes at the zenith of the Digm no longer as a sphere, but as a pulsating arch overflowing from edge to edge and with a colour akin again to violet. It is the anticosmos of the Galaxy, the centre of the forces of Lucifer himself...

The anticosmos of all brahmfaths, and of Shadanakar among them, are two-dimensional: they are like infinite planes. They all intersect each other in the same line; it could be called the demonic axis of the Galaxy...

Two-dimensional layer of Shadanakar is sometimes called hell, but this term here is not quite appropriate: this layer is not the abode of human souls in their postmortality, but the abode of most demonic beings on our planet. You can call it Shadanakara's Anticosmos, but even this is not quite accurate, because the Divine Space is opposed not by this layer alone, but by all demonic worlds, and it is only, so to speak, the main demonic stronghold. His real name is Gashsharva.

Gashsharva is the core of the system created by the demonic forces of Shadanakar, in opposition to the Divine Cosmos, in its supposed substitution". [*Andreev, 2002, p. 158-160*].

Daniel Andreev continues: "The anticosmos of the Galaxy, seen from Digm as a luminary of totally unimaginable and ineffable colour, and from Shogh as a titanic, flaming and pulsating infralighting arch spanning the zenith, from Gasharv appears as if it were a patch of horizon sending an even infralighting glow from infinitely distant spaces...

Here dwell the masters of the lower purgatories, the magmas and the Core - the three sakuals of Vengeance...

The grey ashy complexion of the angels of darkness is repulsive and horrible, and their predatory and ruthless nature is completely exposed in their features. As masters of the lower purgatories, they make up for the loss of their vitality by imbibing the gavvahs of people drawn into the purgatories by their karma...

Completely devoid of humanoidness are the other inhabitants of Gasharva, the magma masters: they are called lynxes. Rather like a moving ridge of hills...

Strangely enough, creatures resembling the proverbial devils do exist and, imagine, even with a tail and horns. They inhabit

Gashsharva and enjoy the dubious pleasure of being the masters of the Core, the sacuala, of Shadanakar's most terrifying afflictions. In fact, it turns out. That many of the legends that we are accustomed to treat with a smile or, at best, seeing in them a symbolic meaning, are to be understood quite literally.

The circle of Gasharva's inhabitants is bizarre and variegated. Of these, I also know some mighty demons of a feminine nature, conventionally called Velgians. They are giants. In the history of mankind they sometimes appear as multipliers of victims and inspirers of anarchy.... Every nation has only one Velga, it seems; in any case, in Russia there is one, very old....

There are other creatures nesting there, but I am not aware of them. But I do know that some of those who were human in Enrophus are there: the bearers of special dark missions. They are hardly affected here, though. The problem is different: in Hashasharva they are carefully prepared by Gagtungr forces for their next incarnation in humanity." [*Andreev, 2002, p. 161-162*].

Daniel Andreev says that "the demonic Base includes another world: the world of one-dimensional space and one-dimensional time. This is the Bottom of Shadanakar, the sufferer of demonic shelters and the few humans who are the bearers of dark missions...

Every brahmfature of our Galaxy has a similar Bottom, except those free of demonic forces; hence, there are millions of such "bottoms" in the Galaxy. And just as two-dimensional cosmic planes cross in a common line, in the same way all cosmic lines of galactic bottoms cross in a single convergence point. This point is in the star system Antares.... A huge planetary system of this star is the centre of god-fighting hordes of the Galaxy, their dwelling place in the three-dimensional world; this is also a titanic metabramphature of demons, the anticosmos of our Milky Way to the extent that this anticosmos generally manifests in the Enroph...

Not only Bottom, but all the worlds of the demonic Base arose, as I have already said, during the cooling of Shadanakar's physical body. Prior to the emergence of organic life in Enroph, Gagtungr's activity was confined to trying to create a layer of habitat for the demonic forces on the surface of the earth, and when that failed, to reinforce and develop Gasharva and other layers associated with the lower crust, with the magmas and with the core of the planet. When organic life emerged in Enrophus, however, its activities were directed towards taking possession of the animal kingdom - this partly succeeded - and towards weighting down the Laws of the Demiurge. As a result of the interaction of these two forces the foundations of those Laws of Nature and Karma in which we live were formed". [*Andreev, 2002, p. 162-164*].

Daniel Andreev explains the activities of the demonic forces of the deep earth: "During the primitive societies demonic forces were busy slowing their development and preparing the layers of transphysical magma and core to receive millions of souls of the coming humanity. Somewhat later, already in historical times, shrasrasras and sakuala uitsrairas were created. Most purgatories arose in even later epochs." [*Andreev, 2002, p. 163*].

Religious studies of Daniel Andreev's religious methods of knowledge, including his metahistorical method and transphysical method, have allowed us to formulate contemporary challenges for the methodology and philosophy of the 21st century diggers in Russia. These include: a) the struggle of the modern Digger against the new ultra-globalist digital society; b) the self-organization of any human being, including Diggers, and the entire living world, which destroys the artificial digital world, since self-organization is possible only in the living world when living creative energy is received from "nowhere" (as atheist philosophers explain), from resonance (as physicists explain), from the divine grace of the Holy Spirit (as theologians explain).

Literature:

1.Andreev D.L. The Rose of the World / D.L. Andreev - Moscow: Mir Uraniya, 2002. - 608 c. ISBN 5-900191-25-7.

Вадим Михайлов
БОРОВИЦКИЙ ХОЛМ
Александровский сад
СПЕЦКАБЕЛЬ
112
К ШАХТЕ
К ТРАССЕ ПРОЕЗДА
ОХРАНА: /ФСО/
СПЕЦБУНКЕР КРЕМЛЯ
СПЕЦКОЛЛЕКТОР
ФАПСИ
ПРЕЗИДЕНТСКОЕ МЕТРО
Таинственный мир подземного Кремля

Diagram of underground space in the Novinsky Boulevard area (up to 300 m depth)
(drawing by V. Mikhailov)

Diagram of the underground cavity beneath Moscow State University on the
Vorobyovy Gory (up to 800 m deep)
(drawing by V. Mikhailov)

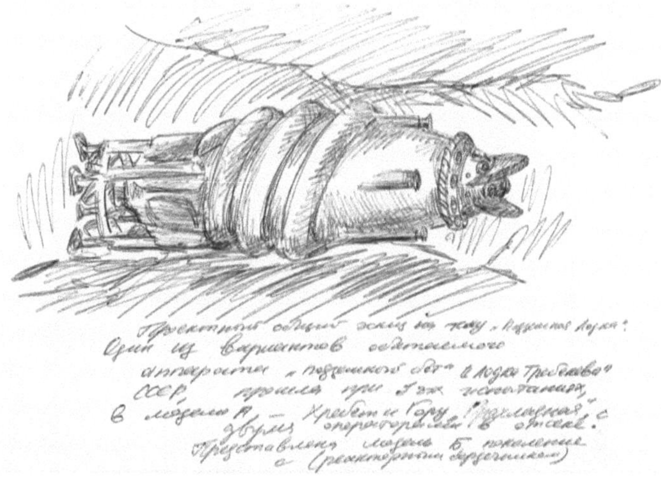

An underground USSR submarine (Trebekov's boat) stranded under
Prokhladnaya Mountain with two operators in the compartment
(drawing by Vadim Mikhailov)

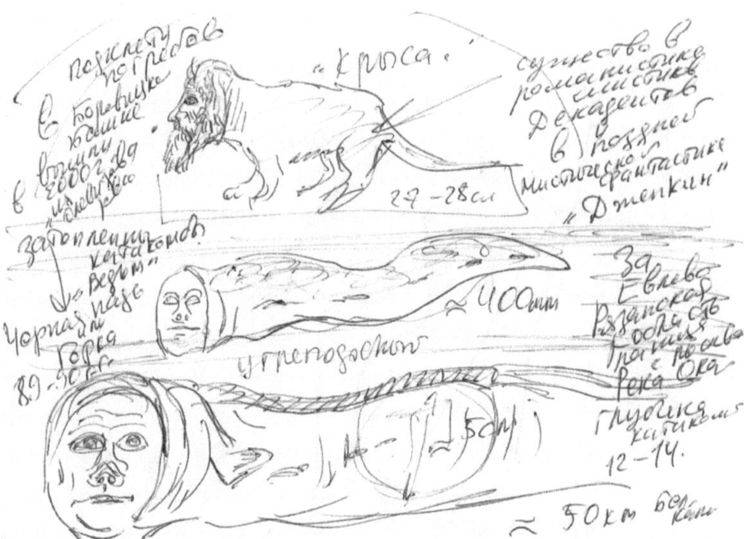

Some of the subterranean creatures: the upper creature found under Borovitsky
Hill in Moscow; the lower creature found in the Ryazan region
(drawing by V. Mikhailov)

Access to Vadim Mikhailov's underground time tunnel in 2007
(drawing by V. Mikhailov)

Vadim Mikhailov's entry into an underground time tunnel from 2007 to the 18th century
(drawing by V. Mikhailov)

I want morebooks!

Buy your books fast and straightforward online - at one of world's fastest growing online book stores! Environmentally sound due to Print-on-Demand technologies.

Buy your books online at
www.morebooks.shop

Kaufen Sie Ihre Bücher schnell und unkompliziert online – auf einer der am schnellsten wachsenden Buchhandelsplattformen weltweit! Dank Print-On-Demand umwelt- und ressourcenschonend produzi ert.

Bücher schneller online kaufen
www.morebooks.shop

Printed by Books on Demand GmbH, Norderstedt / Germany